the

COMMANDMENTS

10

of

FAMILY
BUSINESS
SUCCESSION

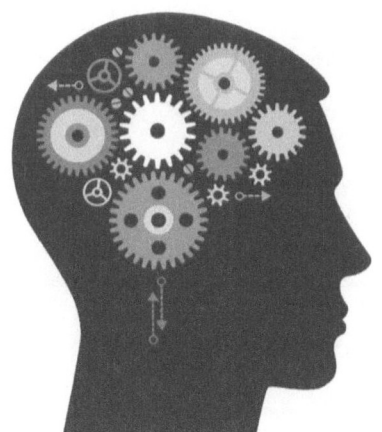

JACOB M. ENGEL

Author *of The Prosperous Leader: How Smart People Achieve Success*

Sept. 2019

By: Jacob M Engel

Author of The Prosperous Leader (www.theprosperousleader.com)

Creator of The Prosperous Courses (www.prosperouscourses.com)

CONTENTS

INTRODUCTION

Why 70% of family businesses never make it to the next generation?

While I know the answer, I'd like to focus on the 30% that do make it! The press covers horror stories of families that don't get along or sue each other in court.

My background is family business, and when I came across the above statistic, I was intrigued about how the 30% managed to pass their businesses down to the next generation.

My research took me to different family businesses across the USA, most more than 1st generation and some 5th generation. I interviewed their CEO's and discovered common practices most use – the secret of their success.

What are the best practices?

- A board that meets continually and holds leadership accountable;

- Formal family meetings discussing family and business; and,

- Strategic planning aligning goals to both family business.

I then found a New York Times article dated August 29, 2001, from a Dr. Astrachan, focusing on these and other predictors of multi-generational succession. Other practices include:

- Requiring family members work outside the business for two to five years before getting a job in the family business;

- Independent board members; and,

- Important decisions like succession planning, salaries, etc., are made by the independent directors.

In my work with family businesses, I also incorporate these and other best practices ensuring multi-generational continuity and, more importantly, prosperity.

For example, I use assessments and evaluations for family members (and others) to ensure we are putting "the right person in the right seat in the right bus," especially for succession.

I emphasize weekly leadership meetings, where we prioritize and review goals, creating both transparency and accountability.

Experts also say that leadership training, culture evaluation, effective communications, etc. all contribute to creating a family business culture allowing both family and non-family to understand their roles and goals and appreciate what each brings to the table.

All organizations must be intentional about their culture and leadership. Otherwise it will go in a direction that no one intended.

I know because it happened to me...

ONE

The First Commandment of Family Business Succession: Plan Early

I was recently invited to meet the owner of a successful family-owned business and his two sons who help run it. They ultimately wanted to know how to prepare the company for the next generation.

Their questions were many:

- "When do we start?"
- "Should the next generation run the company, or should we hire an outside CEO?"
- "How does an advisory board work? How does a family board work?"
- "We are interested in projects outside the family business. Is that a good thing?"
- "What happens if we want to sell?"
- "Can we have all the kids help run the business? How would that work?"
- "How do we share the business equally and fairly without jeopardizing it?"
- "What would retirement look like?"

Planning early is an important aspect of family business succession. It can take years to put everything into place, and the more time you have to plan ahead, the less pressure you create for yourself and others.

Succession planning is a lengthy process because of all the details. You want as much input as possible from trusted advisors, such as lawyers, estate planners, accountants and family business advisors to make great decisions.

Here are some components to think about when setting up a succession plan:

Taxes, Shares, and Assets

How are the shares distributed? To whom, and how much?

How are other assets being distributed? How are those not in the business receiving assets?

What about taxes? Remember the gift tax rules and estate tax ramifications.

If the business owner owns a majority or all of the businesses' shares and doesn't have a proper will in place, at death, the government might enforce the dreaded "death tax." In cities like New York, where you pay federal, state and city tax, this number can be astronomical, forcing the heirs to sell the business or other assets.

With proper planning, this can be mitigated and planned for. Many use life insurance as it's significantly cheaper to buy insurance at an earlier age in good health than later in life.

Moving to a "friendlier" tax state, such as Florida, will mitigate this risk.

Successors

How is the successor(s) being brought in? If they are in the business, how are they being groomed to take over?

This step is usually a lengthy one, requiring lots of contemplation—especially when companies have senior managers in executive positions. How will they react to the next generation, if that's the plan? When will they need to assume full responsibility? If only one family member will take over, how are they chosen over others? Failure to prepare in advance can cause many issues.

A family business owner I know planned five years ahead for this eventual slow-down and succession as CEO. He asked the non-family board members to take an active role in the grooming of his successors, create the plan, and execute it. He retired as chairman of the board, moved to a tax-friendly state, and now comes in for the monthly board meetings.

In a New York Times article, Abby Ellin wrote that the key elements of a successful family business succession are:

• A board that holds family members accountable (especially the CEO) and meets three to six times a year.

• Formal family meetings where the business and family are discussed, at least three times a year.

• A yearly strategic planning event where the company and the family are continually aligned as to what the goals are and what everyone is doing to achieve those goals.

Remember the first commandment of family business succession: Plan early. It takes many years to do it right.

TWO

The Second Commandment of Family Business Succession: Create A Board

Having a board as a private, family business usually seems like a nuisance at best and unnecessary at worst, especially when those board members are outsiders. "Why should strangers know all my problems or how much money I make or lose?"

Most owners of private-owned companies are both officers and board members. They and their family members usually own most if not all of the company shares. No wonder board meetings are almost nonexistent or just a formality.

However, a board is a must, especially if you want to create a seamless succession.

Why?

1. It keeps everyone accountable, as meetings and reports are required.

2. It mitigates politics and allows the company to create a meritocracy, especially with independent directors.

3. It allows for implementation of a seamless succession plan together with continuous updates to the board.

WHAT TYPE OF BOARD WORKS BEST FOR A FAMILY BUSINESS?

There are various types of boards, the most common being the board of directors and board of advisors.

A board of directors has "fiduciary responsibilities" and is held accountable for improper oversight or guidance. They have voting rights and will exercise them as needed. When companies bring in outside investors, the investors might get a seat on the board or insist on becoming independent members. Many family businesses I've worked with initially started off with a board of advisors and gradually morphed into a board of directors.

The purpose and goals of both boards are similar. The question is: what powers does the board of advisors really have? The answer is none, and they can be replaced very easily.

However, because they don't have fiduciary responsibilities, one can attract very talented independent directors, and they will happily serve on the board, usually for a fee. They can bring significant expertise to the table and be a source of knowledge for the company. Plus, with outside guidance from a board, banks feel a lot more comfortable doing business than without a board. Even significant hires will feel reassured when there are outsiders involved.

WHAT SHOULD YOU LOOK FOR IN INDEPENDENT DIRECTORS?

It's wise to stagger independent directors' service periods so they don't all change at once, ensuring continuity. Additionally:

1. They should have family business experience (either having worked in one or advising one).

2. They should have a deep understanding of the issues, such as succession, etc.

3. They should be an open and honest communicator. The board must be able to dissent. It should challenge, probe and ask the tough questions.

4. They should have full integrity.

5. They should be committed to serving.

There are three types of boards: active, passive and hyperactive.

The best board is the active board, which meets regularly. Usually, there's a lead director who is more involved than regular, independent directors. They ask for reports and ask questions.

A passive board meets irregularly and is often unaware of what's happening in the company.

Hyperactive boards are usually the result of a company that has experienced serious turmoil and needs a lot of handholding and guidance.

On one of the boards I served, we initially started as a board of advisors, and then we became a board of directors. We held quarterly meetings with full financial reporting. We helped hire new accountants, lawyers and senior managers. We helped resolve internal conflicts and guided the CEO and his senior team on major issues, etc.

Boards with independent directors can play a very important role in all businesses, especially in family businesses. They create accountability, allow for meritocracy, and are very helpful in a seamless leadership transition.

It should take the lead in the sensitive issues family businesses face when transitioning to the next generation, specifically to ensure that the right successor has been evaluated and given feedback to take on the leadership role.

THREE

The Third Commandment of Family Business Succession: Understand the Family's Rights

I once saw a great line: "Your family has the right to your inheritance but not to run your business."

This topic can cause major misunderstandings and disagreements in family businesses. Often, parents and children have the misconception that a child should automatically be employed by and take over the business.

There are two parts to understanding this situation.

OWNERSHIP VS. MANAGEMENT OR LEADERSHIP

While you may be happy with your children owning all or most of the shares of the company, you might not want them to actually manage it—especially if they don't have the necessary expertise, you have senior managers in place who are doing a great job, or there's competition between the siblings that could cause a serious rift.

(I personally believe that ownership of company shares should be given only to those either in or joining the business. Other assets can be given to those who aren't.)

A family business that I know developed a great plan allowing their children to join the business only after they've worked at another company for at least two years. They also get a nonfamily mentor to teach them the necessary exposure and expertise. In addition, and most importantly, the business's independent directors are heavily involved in the succession process, which includes evaluating and eventually deciding who steps into the leadership role.

I once met with a very successful businessperson who had built a beautiful growing business from scratch. He shared with me his dilemma: A competitor in the same field approached him with an intriguing proposal for them to merge, and he (the person I met with) would become CEO. However, as the competitor had the larger business, he got the larger percentage of shares of the merged company.

All was great until, unfortunately, the majority owner died from a massive heart attack. What they'd overlooked in their agreement was, who inherited his shares. It was his wife and kids, and they insisted on joining the business, even though they didn't have the expertise and too often meddled with the CEO's decisions.

I asked him whether he had a board, and he said no, but I wasn't the only one who had asked him, so he was putting one together. I also suggested he have independent directors, not only his accountant, attorney, etc., and they should decide who joined the business and in what capacity.

Make sure your family knows and understands your business's succession plan and policy very clearly because this can eliminate many headaches down the road.

Ensuring that Family Members Want to be Involved

One of the greatest legacies a business founder can leave behind is family members who carry on his or her dream in a way that will shine a positive light on the mission and vision of the business. Having family members enthusiastic about joining the business is typically a prerequisite for this to happen.

A friend who's a family business psychologist (yes, there is such a thing) told me a great story that involved a family business the parents were very eager for the kids to join, but the kids were very reluctant. They finally met with this psychologist, and he asked the kids why they weren't interested in joining. They answered very simply that they'd seen too many other situations where family members joined a family business, and there was sibling rivalry, so the parents eventually weren't happy, and neither were the kids. So rather than going from a happy, successful family to an unhappy one, they elected to forgo the choice.

My friend suggested the parents create a board and hire him to work on this issue with a time frame for the kids to decide whether they saw a way to work together. Having a board and a person with family business expertise can ensure that both parents and kids feel their concerns and needs are listened to and being dealt with.

Sadly, as mentioned 70% of family businesses don't make it to the second generation, and even less make it to the third. As the proverbial saying goes, many businesses will go from "shirtsleeves to shirtsleeves in three generations."

How can you ensure that your family business is part of the 30% or less that succeed?

Having a clear and well-thought-out plan, a competent board with independent board members, and the right family members involved in business management can ensure a seamless and successful transition to future generations.

FOUR

The Fourth Commandment of Family Business Succession: Have A Life Outside the Business

I once met a prominent family business psychologist, and he shared with me a very powerful insight. He often gets called into family businesses to help with the family's business succession plan. One of the things he insists on is meeting the spouse of the founder, owner or CEO. If he ascertains that the only reason the spouse has respect for the founder is because of their position, he claims that the founder will likely never retire, as they won't want to lose the power of the title. Therefore, a seamless business succession will likely never happen.

Having a life outside the family business is important for so many reasons, especially if you want to have a smooth succession.

A Reason to Retire

Having hobbies, philanthropic endeavors, community activities and family interests keeps you from being a slave to your business or feeling chained to your desk. When the founder or business owner is so wrapped up in the business they can't separate their identity from it, they'll likely find a reason for not stepping away in a timely, seamless manner.

Oftentimes, founders are so afraid to step back from their business they use a variety of excuses, like saying their kids or managers aren't ready (even if they've been running the business for years), they're not ready to retire, or they're afraid to step out of their comfort zone.

In his book The 8th Habit: From Effectiveness to Greatness, Stephen Covey wrote, "Retire from your job but never from meaningful projects. If you want to live a long life, you need eustress, that is, a deep sense of meaning and of contribution to worthy projects and causes, particularly, your intergenerational family." In other words, have great and inspiring interests and projects that will fill you with energy to retire to.

A good friend who's the former CEO of a large family business told me that when his grandfather founded the business, it was predicated on the understanding that before retirement age, the family member in charge would help the next generation take over. My friend decided at age 62 to start the process and removed himself as CEO, becoming the chairman of the board to help the next generation assume the CEO position.

My friend enjoys his hobbies immensely—he's a community activist, a religious leader, an independent board member for other family businesses, etc. He's never bored and enjoys his retirement. His outside interests and understanding of the succession process gave him the satisfaction and courage to step away and enjoy his other endeavors as much as he enjoyed running his business. And his stepping away allowed the next generation to move into the leadership role in a progressive and systematic way with his guidance and mentoring.

OPENING YOURSELF UP TO NEW POSSIBILITIES

Stanford professor Carol Dweck in her excellent book Mindset: The New Psychology of Success explains that people either have a growth or fixed mindset. If you say things like, "Oh, I'm just not good at math," or "I'm not good with technology," it's because you believe you have a finite amount of wisdom (IQ) and it can't be changed. This is a fixed mindset.

On the other hand, if you say things like, "Maybe at the moment I don't understand it, but I'm willing to give it a try and learn something new," that is a growth mindset. For many, this attitude comes from childhood and being led to believe that either you're good at something or not.

Try to cultivate a growth mindset to open yourself up to new possibilities other than being stuck in your business. Be bold, and great things may happen. A great question you might want to ask yourself is: "What new things would I be doing if money weren't an issue and I couldn't fail?" The fear of failure is what Dweck says holds many of us back from trying to learn new things.

Taking on new hobbies, learning new languages, listening to new music, traveling to new places, etc., rather than just focusing on your business gives the younger generation space to grow into their positions. The easiest way for the next generation to be successful in assuming a leadership role is doing it intentionally and proactively. Otherwise, it often becomes contentious and has a negative effect on the morale of the team.

Your family business's future leaders will also probably love you for being a great role model for their own eventual retirement. Regularly stepping out of your comfort zone can help you build new neural pathways in your brain and keep your brain flexible as you age. Scientists call this ability to change your brain "neuroplasticity."

A family member retired at age 65 from a prominent banking executive position, and many thought this might be the beginning of the end for him. Instead, he reinvented his passion for writing and is a prolific editor and writer. He's well into his 80s and going strong.

There's a great saying that goes: "The best time to plant a tree was 20 years ago. The second-best time is now." If you haven't started cultivating a life outside your business until now, don't give up, just start today.

Mark Victor Hansen, co-creator of the Chicken Soup for the Soul book series, wrote a great book called How to Make the Rest of Your Life the Best of Your Life. Read it, and make it happen. Doing so can benefit both you and your family business.

FIVE

The Fifth Commandment of Family Business Succession: Know Whether to Sell or Transfer

M any founders struggle with the big question: "Do I sell the family business, or do I look to transfer it to the next generation?"

There are great benefits to selling, and there are many ways a sale can be accomplished. It allows the founder to cash in the chips and retire without a second thought of social security benefits or Medicare. It allows them to pursue dreams and well-earned, once-in-a-lifetime payouts.

However, given that you have enough years to enjoy it, the money still has to make money, especially if you want to leave substantial amounts to your heirs or your favorite charity.

I know many founders who sold their business and regretted it immensely. For some, the business was the love of their life and they missed it. For others, it was usually when the investors sold the business for even greater multiples that they felt a twinge of regret. For many, it's mainly because they don't feel they can continue the business into the next generation and do it right—not always about the money.

SELLING

I've seen some astute founders take advantage of what is called a "second bite at the apple," meaning, they will find a minority investor, usually a strategic one (the difference between a strategic investor versus a private equity investor is very important), where both parties make sure they feel very comfortable working with each other for a period of time. Then there is an agreement to a larger-share purchase within a certain amount of years at an agreed-upon multiple of earnings, where the founder has the option to buy back the investor/partner. This way, if the business really takes off and the owner is agreeable to the terms of the second sale, he will reap the benefit of a larger payout. Otherwise, he must be agreeable to buy the investors out, as most investors want a clear exit plan.

If an owner doesn't believe their heirs are capable or interested, or strategic or PE buyers aren't willing to offer what he thinks it's worth, there are other possibilities to explore. Perhaps he has a great team of employees who are like family to him and are interested in running the business.

In this instance, he can sell to the employees, known as an employee sale ownership plan (ESOP). It's a way for both the owner to get his money and the business to continue. There are many rules to an ESOP, and it must be done right, as it's very hard to undo.

Another option, if there are other partners involved, is to do either a "buy me, buy you" (BMBY) or a buyout, if one partner predeceases another. BMBY works well when equal partners decide to allow one partner to buy out the other's shares. One party will name a price and the other party has the right to either buy or sell at that price. This keeps everyone honest and the agreement fair.

If one partner predeceases the other and they allow for a buyout in their agreement, then a formula should be included in the agreement (e.g., multiple of earnings, etc.) based on current evaluations or a negotiated price. (One word of caution: Many times, a price is set in the agreement subject to revision on a yearly basis, but nobody remembers to update the price!)

TRANSFERRING

If the founder decides a sale is not an option and wants to keep the business for the next generation, there are many ways to make it work. If the next generation is willing and capable, that makes it easier, given the owners have planned early, created a board, know their rights and have created a life outside the business.

Since there are many ways to structure a continuation, you will need both an estate attorney and an accountant familiar with tax issues, and to have your will and all documents executed and signed correctly. Many founders are afraid of writing or signing their will, but an unwritten or unsigned will is a recipe for disaster. Wills and agreements also need to be revisited continuously, as laws change.

If there are other partners or family members involved, that will require making sure everyone is on board and that the proper documents reflect that agreement. All these documents should be written and executed on by an expert.

In short, make sure you know your options, talk to the experts, make a decision and execute properly.

Six

The Sixth Commandment of Family Business Succession: Evaluate A Successor

E valuating a successor is one of the most (if not the most) difficult challenges of any CEO, especially in a family-owned business. In fact, it's been said that the test of a successful CEO is how well he or she brings on a successor.

The challenges can be numerous; I will enumerate some of the more common ones.

The current CEO hasn't decided to move up or move on

This means they are still undecided on if and when to make a move, usually up as chairman or out.

Successor CEOs, especially talented ones, do not want to wait in the wings for indefinite amounts of time. Often in such cases, the good CEOs leave and there is a power grab between siblings or other family members.

There are multiple family members involved in the business and more than one believes they are candidates

Alternatively, other family (or non-family) members may not be aware of the succession plan or are not happy with the choice.

This will create either a power struggle or a power vacuum, both detrimental to the business. In both cases, the smoother the transition, the less stress it puts on the company and its employees. Employees need to feel safe, (see Maslow's pyramid), psychological safety included. If they experience too much uncertainty or internal struggles, eventually, they will also leave.

Pay and authority are not agreed upon

Pay in a family business is a sensitive topic fraught with danger. There are a few different ways pay can be constructed in a family business, but too often, it's emotion-based, not meritocracy based. It should be the latter and set by the board. That same board will usually hire the new CEO and create a pay package with incentives.

How Are You Choosing Your Successor?

According to Dr. David Keirsey in Please Understand Me, certain personalities are either more suitable or not suitable for leadership.

While I'm not trying to get into a debate about whether leaders are born or made, according to Keirsey, it's more inborn than learned. Certain inborn personalities have a greater draw and success toward leadership, as the characteristics of great leadership are creating the vision, implementing it, and holding people accountable.

Not every person can create a vision, or the right vision, especially if they are not big-picture oriented. Not every person can implement a vision, especially if they are scattered and unfocused. Not every person can hold people accountable in the right way, especially if they are forgiving and soft by nature. While nature is only part of who we are, it does play a significant role, according to Keirsey.

The other part is our nurture or learned behaviors. This means if we have dysfunctional or inconsistent behaviors such as moodiness, anger, or other habits like talking and not listening or being very demanding or demeaning, these all make for bad leadership.

Today, many companies are big believers in testing for emotional intelligence (EQ).

EQ, according to Professor Daniel Goleman, is the ability to:

1. Recognize, understand and manage our own emotions.

2. Recognize, understand and influence the emotions of others.

When choosing a successor, you want to incorporate experience, knowledge of the industry, and the ability to lead as a litmus test. In order to achieve that, you need a few critical things in place.

As I mentioned in my previous articles, the first is a succession plan. The earlier you start, the easier and better the succession.

Then, you need to have a board to help evaluate the successor and guide him/her through the many steps needed to fit into the CEO's shoes. A coach can be helpful during the transition and have the successor go through specific trainings. There are also some great family business institutes that will help family businesses in their succession planning.

The board should then be transparent about their decision making and work alongside other family members and senior managers to ensure buy-in. Remember, plan early, have a board, assess the candidates, train and enjoy the process!

SEVEN

The Seventh Commandment of Family Business Succession: Don't Create Competition

Many family businesses create internal competition for the top job, the idea being it's survival of the fittest. However, this creates friction between the contenders. While in other companies, those who don't get the top job will leave, in a family business, if they leave, it creates resentment and acrimonious relationships. Even if they do decide to stay, it creates tension and disharmony.

A company I was working with had two candidates it was promoting for the top job. The problem was that they didn't get along with each other. This created an internal competition unhelpful for the company and the candidates. It became so intense that a third-party professional, had to step in. While he worked for six months to get the two candidates to work together, it had created a disharmony that was hard to overcome.

The following 10 steps can help ensure your family business is putting forth the best candidates and that everyone will enjoy the process.

1. HAVE INDEPENDENT MEMBERS OF THE BOARD OVERSEE THE SUCCESSION PLAN.

Boards with independent directors that have family business expertise mitigate the conflict and allow each person to shine. They help everyone understand the roles and goals of each person and help them find their best spot in the company. As Jim Collins famously said in his book, Good to Great: Why Some Companies Make the Leap... And Others Don't, you must make sure you have the right people on the right bus and in the right seat. This is even more critical for family members!

2. Have the candidate(s) report to non-family members.

Having family members report to non-family members will allow them to be coached and mentored without them feeling undue pressure from their father/uncle/brother, etc.

3. Develop the candidate's leadership skills.

Leaders are both born and made. This person should ultimately relish the role and have the right skill sets to be a leader. Most, if not all, leadership skills are what we call "soft skills" and are rarely taught in schools, homes or businesses, yet are so critical for growth and success.

According to a study by Google-named Project Oxygen, in which it surveyed its own employees for 10 years, leaders who have coaching capabilities and soft skills or emotional intelligence were viewed as the highest-performing managers.

Encourage the candidate to take courses, attend seminars, read books, listen to podcasts, etc. so they can further enhance their soft skills and grow into the role. Connecting them with a leadership coach is also a helpful option, as a coach can help them understand their strengths and abilities, especially as a leader.

4. Create a meritocracy so that people understand how leaders are chosen.

Creating a meritocracy is especially challenging in a family business, though it's essential. What happens if one or more family members are laggards? Do you fire them? What if members are not in the right seat? Do you move them up or down? If family members aren't held to the same standards as other managers, it will create resentment between the non-family managers. That leads me to my next point.

5. Create transparency and accountability for all.

No sacred cows or favorites! This might require better hiring policies, even within the family. It's better than having unfit people in a job because other circumstances are ideal.

6. Give equal opportunity to all senior managers to present to the board.

Allowing all managers, including family, to present to the board gives everyone the right exposure and enhances transparency. It evens out the playing field so everyone has a shot.

7. Allow the candidates to prove their leadership skills in various projects or initiatives.

Give family members and managers the opportunity to jump into projects. This allows them to shine and learn new parts of the business. I recall in my own career in the family business, we had decided to move our systems to an advanced enterprise resource-planning system. I was asked to plan and implement the system even though I did not have a background in computers. It took me about a year-and-a-half of hard work to get it up and running, yet despite the challenge, it was one of the best things I could have done for the company and for myself. I learned so much about how processes were being done, the financials, managing inventory, Crystal reporting, etc.

8. Allow them to work outside the business, preferably before joining.

Some family businesses won't allow family members to join unless they have some experience working in a similar business. It's a great idea. Having previous or outside experience allows the family member to join with some understanding of the basics and how businesses run.

9. Have them join a family business institute.

Family institutes are a great way to meet other family members with the same intergenerational business issues. It exposes them to experts in the field, proven techniques, and ideas, plus it's a great place for referrals if needed.

10. Have a family council to deal with non-business matters.

Often, there are assumptions family members not in the business make about the business, especially spouses. Having everyone hear the same message and information through a reliable channel, such as a family council, will be extremely beneficial.

Open communication between all family members is paramount to keeping the peace. In a family business, peace between the members is key to long-term succession.

EIGHT

The Eighth Commandment of Family Business Succession: Make the Rest of Your Life the Best of Life

Retirement should not be a death sentence. It should be the opportunity to re-invent yourself, do the things you have never done before but always secretly wished for, learn new things, travel, join new classes, and the list goes on.

The first pre-requisite is to have a positive outlook on your new phase in life. This usually requires having a positive outlook on everything. Here are two very different people I know and their responses to retirement.

Both retirees had very successful careers—money was not an issue—and both had loving families.

Yet one was forever miserable and burdensome while the other was full of life and looking at the opportunities ahead.

That's because one made the effort to enjoy every moment and continuously feel blessed while the other was always complaining or criticizing.

What are some of the factors that created these two different scenarios?

The one we'll call Mark was very money-driven and materialistic-minded.

For Mark, the mark of success (pun intended) was how much money or "stuff" he had or was worth. It created a scarcity mentality, meaning if someone else had something, he had less. He, therefore, couldn't share his wealth or his love.

His outlook in life was based on himself first and everyone else last.

By the time retirement came around, he was so attached to his business he couldn't step away and had to be forced out by his own children. Mark also never cherished his family, so by the time he did have time on his hands, nobody was interested in building a relationship with him.

He died with millions of unspent dollars in his account and an estate that was inherited by those he could have built a loving relationship with had he been less tight-fisted and more generous.

Contrast that with Barbara, who, while a very successful entrepreneur who worked hard to build a business, she never lost sight of her "raison d'etre" and showing how much she cared about her family and community. If anything, it was others first, then herself.

She was very charitable and funded many community projects. She had many hobbies and was as content being involved in those projects as much as running her business. She had an abundance mentality, meaning if others were successful, she was happy for their success and was happiest when she could share with others.

She taught her family that having values was more important than money and sharing with others was mandatory.

Her preparation for retirement was a series of taking long trips away from the business, empowering others to take on leadership roles, mentoring others to start and run their own businesses, and leaving a legacy of charity and love that memorialized her name to her family, friends and community members.

Rabbi Harold Kushner is popularly attributed for the quote "Nobody on their deathbed has ever said 'I wish I had spent more time at the office.'"

A family business CEO who transitioned to the fifth generation shared with me their secret to success, based on some key fundamental principles that perpetuate the family legacy.

1. Stewardship: The responsibility to maintain and enhance the assets for the next generation.

2. Service: The obligation to be of service to both the family and the community. It means always giving back to the community that was part of your success.

3. Charity: If ever the company—or even part of the company—is

sold, a certain percentage (40%) is put into a charitable foundation for future charity work.

If you are blessed with financial success, health, and the ability to have an impact on others, this is the greatest gift. Use it to the max. There are so many ways to be of service as a retiring family business owner. You can mentor young entrepreneurs or join SCORE, the Small Business Administration's mentoring service. You can teach or visit schools, hospitals, nursing homes, prisons, etc. You can chime in on social media discussions in your areas of expertise (If you don't know how, ask your child/grandchild/niece/nephew/next-door neighbor, etc.), or join a 55-plus community to get to know people who are in the same place in life as you are.

In what other ways could you make the rest of your life the best of your life?

NINE

The Ninth Commandment–Teach thy values to your children/family.

Recently, I was involved in a few family businesses that the founders were values driven and not money driven. They were into giving back to their communities, even when they didn't have much to share. They were ethical, honest, upstanding citizens and yet after their passing, their family business descended into the abyss of deceit and bitter inter-familial dysfunctional relationships.

Did not the founders believe that family values and business ethics are important? Of course they did!

Why did the family members toss them out the window? Disregarding the important messages they were to have learned and integrated into their lives and into the business!

In the late 1800's or early 1900's a peddler immigrated in the to the USA from Eastern Europe and was able to start a small pushcart business. (For those unfamiliar with the term 'pushcart', it was a cart on wheels that was pushed around and peddlers would sell their wares on these carts).

The pushcart eventually became a store that eventually became a large and successful chain.

The founder was of the Jewish faith and built his business with faith-based values.

The "TEN COMMANDMENTS" were sacrosanct.

Family values were holy, the day of rest was a day of rest with prayers and families, and gathering for meals was part and parcel of their DNA.

One of the unique customs the founder committed to was keeping his stores closed for the Sabbath and Jewish holidays.

If you think back to the early 1900's, it was quite an accomplishment, but it showed his employees, Jewish and non-Jewish alike, that faith was nonnegotiable and a core value.

The founder, getting on in age, wrote down his values and incorporated them into the company's DNA.

His concern was that, while the Sabbath was a day of rest and the stores were closed, they weren't closed on the Jewish holidays. He wanted to ensure the stores would be closed on the holidays, so he put it into the charter of the company... that on holidays the stores were to be closed.

Years have gone by, the descendants of the founder eventually weren't as committed as the founder, but as the company charter was to be closed on the holiday's nobody dared to change the founder's wish.

However, ironically they decided that the Sabbath was a very important business day and as the founder never explicitly included the Sabbath in the charter, they started to keep the stores open on the Sabbath.

What I learned from this story is that while the founder(s) were keen on imparting their values they never thought that they needed to share their very basic beliefs!

They believed that it was a given.

But as someone once said, it's all common sense that is not so common. Or it's common sense but not common practice!

My very dear friend Paul Silberberg, former President of CMS, shared with me his grandmother's ethical will. The power of the will was that it spelled out everything that she believed was important to her and to her next of kin.

I believe the success of their family is that ethical will, as it imparted her most important family values to her family.

I will share a part of the will, as it's so impactful.

To my beloved family: children, grandchildren, and great-grandchildren,

I am a simple Jewish woman. I believe in the eternal truths of our Torah; I believe in the Living G-d; I believe in the ultimate destiny of Israel; and I believe, with all my heart and soul, in the sanctity of the family.

Your Pop and I lived our lives in accordance with these ideals and we tried, by word and deed, to teach them to you. I am proud of your response.

Since Pop left us, my life has been lonely and in recent years, filled with physical pain and suffering.

In spite of this, I think of myself as blessed by Almighty G-d to have all of you near me, and to receive and accept the constant expressions of your love. No one can fully understand the joy and happiness I feel when you call, when you visit and, most of all, when you join together in family celebration.

Your Pop died with dignity, surrounded by his beloved family. I do not know whether I will be so blessed, or where or when my time will come. Whatever the circumstances, I am ready, and I will go with a full heart, secure in the knowledge that my (Shema Koleinu) prayers have been answered.

So—now it is time to say our last goodbyes—may G-d bless you, and keep you, and watch over you all your days, and may you be forever warmed by my eternal love.

—Grandma

My point is that as founders or even next generations of the founders, your family must hear again and again the values that are sacrosanct and the commitment to those values, otherwise they will decide what they believe you meant, whether you meant it, or not.

Don't leave your values up for interpretation!

As the saying goes "Repeat, Rinse, Repeat..." your values, your ethics, your integrity, so that it remains for eternity.

TEN

The Tenth Commandment

I know I'm harping a lot on this subject and maybe it's because I see so many people mistakenly believe that they can control everything including their kids from their grave, so they create complex wills!

They mistakenly believe that their children, left to their own devices, will play nice with their siblings and with other family members, especially with a lot of money at stake...

They mistakenly believe that nobody in their right mind will sue brothers/sisters in court.

Most importantly, they mistakenly believe that their family will be appreciative and grateful to the deceased for leaving them significant assets and money.

However, the more money there is, the higher potential fights and disagreements.

The bigger the business the more enticement for foul play and cheating.

As the saying goes, "Power and money corrupts and huge fortunes with absolute power corrupts absolutely."

Many if not most estate attorneys are great in helping people save taxes but not very great in helping them save the family!

The big question is, can families live and play nicely together? Can family and business coexist? Can it bring out the best in the family members? Can all employees feel like family and not feel threatened by family members?

The answer is a resounding yes, but it needs to be intentional and well planned out.

Here are some practical tips of how other families created a legacy of family unity, respect for the deceased and their values, a sharing of pride for their hard work, and the continuation of family mission and vision that future generations can share with each other.

One large family instituted a yearly camp for over 600 members of their extended family. They share about the business, their charitable endeavors, and ensure the family understands the founders' legacy.

One founder even setup a separate fund so that the extended family gets together at least once a year.

Some families have setup tuition funds for all members.

Many have created charity foundations and encourage family members to participate in community work.

Another wrote a family business handbook, like an employee handbook, every family member gets so they understand the importance of joining the family business and the rules they must abide by.

Leaving money and businesses to the next generation can be a very effective tool for continuing the legacy, but only if done right.

Warren Buffett said it well, that he's leaving enough money to his kids so they can do anything but not so much they can do nothing!

Remember these Ten Commandments for creating the legacy you wish to perpetuate:

Be intentional.

Create a unifying mission and vision for your family.

Implement the mission and vision.

Make sure family members understand and buy in to the mission and vision.

Make it personal to each member.

Create a mentoring program for the younger generations (when you're not there anymore).

Clarify the values that the family stands for.

Hold people accountable to those values.

Every event should remind people of values and mission.

Live the life that encompasses and demonstrates all the above!

In closing, I just came across a letter from the famous T. Boone Pickens, who passed away on Sept. 11th. Here is the critical part.

"In my final months, I came to the sad reality that my life really did have a fourth quarter and the clock really would run out on me. I took the time to convey some thoughts that reflect back on my rich and full life.

One question I was asked time and again: What is it that you will leave behind?

I've long recognized the power of effective communication. That's why in my later years I began to reflect on the many life lessons I learned along the way, and shared them with all who would listen.

Fortunately, I found the young have a thirst for this message. Many times over the years, I was fortunate enough to speak at student commencement ceremonies, and that gave me the chance to look out into a sea of the future and share some of these thoughts with young minds. My favorite of these speeches included my grandchildren in the audience.

It's your shot now.

If I had to single out one piece of advice that's guided me through life, most likely it would be from my grandmother, Nellie Molonson. She always made a point of making sure I understood that on the road to success, there's no point in blaming others when you fail.

Never forget where you come from. I honored the values my family instilled in me, and was honored many times over by the success they allowed me to achieve.

I also long practiced what my mother preached to me throughout her life—be generous. Those values came into play throughout my career, but especially so as my philanthropic giving exceeded my substantial net worth in recent years.

For most of my adult life, I've believed that I was put on Earth to make money and be generous with it. I've never been a fan of inherited wealth.

I liked knowing that I helped a lot of people. I received letters every day thanking me for what I did, the change I fostered in other people's lives. Those people should know that I appreciated their letters.

My wealth was built through some key principles, including:

Change creates opportunity.

Have faith, both in spiritual matters and in humanity, and in yourself. That faith will see you through the dark times we all navigate.

I left an undying love for America, and the hope it presents for all. I left a passion for entrepreneurship, and the promise it sustains. I left the belief that future generations can and will do better than my own.

Thank you. It's time we all move on.

ELEVEN

What's Next?

Thomas Edison supposedly said, "Vision without execution is just hallucination."

What I'd like to share with you is a simple yet very powerful tool that will show you how to execute every day on your vision.

I will do the first one so that you can then easily follow it for the next ones.

If you get stuck, feel free to email me and I will be glad to help!

Plan early:

Planning early is always a great way to accomplish any goal as it takes away from the stress of executing a last-minute plan. Many people say, "I just do things so much better when I do it last minute!" There is some truth to this line of thinking, though mostly there is a reason why we procrastinate and its usually not a great one. It's either because we have a hard time deciding what we want to do, or we have a hard time committing in general.

This exercise, which I call GSAP, is a great way to put everything on paper. Then you can decide what you are doing and when. Instead of making emotional decisions before the facts, you first get the facts on paper and then make the emotional decision!

GSAP stands for Goals-Strategies-Action Plan.

Let's say your goal is to have a succession plan in place within 5 years.

GOAL: Succession plan in 5 years...

Strategies: We can have multiple strategies for accomplishing this goal.

- Talk to experts that understand the process well. (estate lawyers, family business coaches/consultants, independent (family business) directors, other family businesses, and join a Family Business Institute, etc.).

- Read books, articles, podcasts, etc. that talk about succession planning.

- Find seminars that specifically talk about succession.

- All of the above…

Action Plan:

1-6 months: Become very knowledgeable about the subject of succession planning.

6-12 months: Decide which experts you feel comfortable working with and that you will trust to give you open and honest advice.

1-2 years: Start meeting with each team member to create your board of advisors, eventually having them all sit at one table to discuss the plan.

2-3 years: Meet with your team and start sharing important information about your company. It's very important for you to get comfortable meeting and sharing.

3-4 years: Discuss your challenges if any and your succession plan. Have an Action Plan to start the process of succession (Create the same GSAP model for them as well).

4-5 years: Start implementing the plan with the team being part of the implementation process.

There are no shortcuts to any good and well thought out plan. It requires step by step actions to make it happen.

The same will go for the other "Commandments" listed above!

If you need resources such as names of advisors, lawyers or coaches, I have many names I've worked with over the years and I'm happy to share.

If you're ready to begin planning for your business succession, I want to help you along the way.

I want to take you through the first steps.

Contact me at Jacob@theprosperousleader.com for a free consultation.